LESLEY WATERS

Starters

LESLEY WATERS

Starters

Photography by Philip Wilkins

WEIDENFELD & NICOLSON

Lesley Waters

Lesley Waters, a former chef and cookery demonstrator, is now a popular television cook who appears regularly on *Ready Steady Cook* and *Who'll Do the Pudding?*

After training in London and Germany Lesley joined Prue Leith's Restaurant and was quickly promoted to senior chef. Following a period as a freelance chef and caterer she joined Leith's School of Food and Wine as an instructor, where she perfected her cookery demonstration and food photography skills.

Lesley has worked in television since 1989. In addition to *GMTV* and *Bazaar,* she has been resident cook for Lifestyle Channel and for UK Living. In 1992 she teamed up with Malcolm Gluck to present the *Superplonk* video, the guide to top supermarket wines. In 1994 she co-presented a 12-part series for Anglia TV about healthy living called *Bodyworks*. During 1996 she was one of the main presenters of *Can't Cook Won't Cook* and she is currently part of the teams on *Ready Steady Cook* for BBC2, *Who'll Do the Pudding?* for BBC1 and *Mixing It* for Channel 5.

Lesley is a qualified aerobics instructor and has recently become a mother. Her books include *Ready Steady Cook 3, Bazaar Hearty Eater, Fifteen-Minute Feasts* and *Four Seasons Cookery* for BBC Books, *Weight Watchers Carefree Christmas, Weight Watchers Storecupboard Cookery* and Sainsbury's *Quick and Easy Food for Friends*.

Contents

MARINATED VODKA SALMON 10

PEAR AND PEAR SALAD 12

VERMOUTH MUSSELS ON FENNEL STEAKS 14

WHITE BEAN PÂTÉ WITH HORSERADISH 16

PAN-FRIED CHICKEN LIVERS WITH CARAMELIZED RED ONIONS 18

FLAT MUSHROOMS ON LINGUINI 20

GAZPACHO SALAD 22

ORIENTAL BROTH 24

Salami ravigotte 26

Mezze plate 28

Honeyed duck with papaya salsa 30

Crab tarts with ginger pistou 32

The basics 34

Start as you mean to go on,

'keep it simple'.

Introduction

Invariably if I go to a restaurant these days I find myself ordering a feast from the list of first courses. Perhaps this is because I have a healthy appetite, but it is also because I always find the starters the most interesting and imaginative section of the menu. Gone are the days of the predictable melon or prawn cocktail. Starters now mean exciting morsels which are served warm, hot or cold, combining different food cultures and flavours, to create a mouthwatering selection equal to any main course.

Here I have put together some of my favourites, such as a gazpacho salad, an aromatic crab tart with ginger pistou and a delicious plate of mezze. All these recipes make wonderful first courses, but are just as good served as lunches, brunches or supper dishes for any occasion.

Lesley Waters

MARINATED VODKA SALMON

SERVES 4

225 g/8 oz salmon fillet in
    one piece, cut on a slant
    lengthways into very thin
    slices
salt and pepper
1 shallot, finely chopped
juice of 1 lemon
3 tablespoons vodka
2 tablespoons extra virgin
    olive oil
½ bunch of dill tips

Place the salmon slices on a large serving plate and season well.

In a bowl, mix together the shallot, lemon juice and vodka. Pour over the salmon and leave to marinate for 30 minutes.

To serve, drizzle the olive oil over the salmon and sprinkle with the dill tips. Serve at once with crispbreads or melba toasts.

Continue the meal with venison ragout and a purée of root vegetables, such as potato and celeriac.

Pear and pear salad

SERVES 4

1 large or 2 small ripe avocados,
    sliced
mixed baby salad leaves
4 tablespoons olive oil
175 g/6 oz smoked bacon, diced
1 tablespoon white wine vinegar
2 teaspoons coarsegrain
    mustard
1 large or 2 small ripe dessert
    pears, cored and sliced
salt and pepper

Arrange the avocado slices and some salad leaves on four large serving plates.

In a large frying pan, heat the olive oil. Add the bacon and fry until crisp. Add the vinegar, mustard and pear slices to the pan, season to taste and briefly heat through. Spoon the bacon and pears over the salad leaves and avocado and serve at once.

Wild mushroom risotto would be the perfect main course after this starter. Finish with some Brie or Roquefort cheese.

VERMOUTH MUSSELS
on fennel steaks

SERVES 4

900 g/2 lb fresh mussels
2 fennel bulbs, trimmed and
     thickly sliced
olive oil for brushing
salt and pepper
50 g/2 oz butter
150 ml/5 fl oz dry vermouth
1 garlic clove, crushed
1 bunch of flat-leaf parsley,
     roughly chopped

Clean the mussels by scrubbing well and rinsing in several changes of cold water. Pull away the 'beards' or seaweed-like threads and discard any mussels that are cracked or that do not close when tapped.

Steam the fennel for 10 minutes or until just tender. Dry well on paper towels. Brush generously with olive oil and season well. Heat a chargrill pan or heavy frying pan and fry the fennel for 8–10 minutes on each side until very brown.

Melt the butter in a large saucepan. Add the mussels, vermouth, garlic and half the parsley. Season well. Bring to a simmer, cover the pan with a tight-fitting lid and leave to steam over a medium heat for 4–5 minutes or until the mussels' shells have opened. (Discard any mussels that remain closed.)

Arrange the fennel steaks on four serving plates and spoon the mussels with all their juices over the top. Scatter with the remaining parsley and serve at once.

Follow this with lamb meatballs with a mint and coriander sauce, then a raspberry pie served with crème fraîche.

WHITE BEAN PÂTÉ
with horseradish

SERVES 4

2 x 400 g/14 oz cans of butter
   beans, drained and rinsed
4 teaspoons creamed
   horseradish
5 tablespoons olive oil
grated zest and juice of 1 lime
salt and pepper
175g/6 oz broad beans,
   cooked and peeled
2 tablespoons flat-leaf parsley
   leaves (left whole)

Put three-quarters of the butter beans in a food processor with the horseradish, 4 tablespoons of the olive oil, the lime zest and plenty of salt and pepper. Blend until smooth and creamy, adding a little warm water if necessary.

In a small bowl, toss the remaining butter beans and the broad beans with the lime juice, parsley leaves and the remaining olive oil. Season to taste.

Pile the creamy pâté into a shallow serving dish and scatter over the bean relish. Grind over plenty of black pepper and serve with warm crusty bread or chill until required.

For a main course I might serve hot paprika chicken with fruity salsa.

PAN-FRIED CHICKEN LIVERS
with caramelized red onions

SERVES 4

450 g/1 lb chicken livers,
  trimmed
300 ml/10 fl oz milk
2 red onions, halved and cut
  into wedges
3 tablespoons olive oil
25 g/1 oz butter
3 tablespoons brandy
½ baguette
1 bunch of watercress, washed

Place the chicken livers and milk in a bowl and leave to soak for 30 minutes.

Brush the onion wedges with olive oil and place under a low grill for about 15 minutes or until softened and lightly charred.

Drain the chicken livers and pat dry on paper towels. In a frying pan, heat the oil and butter until lightly foaming. Add the livers and fry for 3−4 minutes or until just cooked. Remove the pan from the heat and add the brandy.

Meanwhile, slice the baguette on a slant, allowing 2 slices per person. Lightly toast the slices and arrange on four plates.

To serve, top the baguette slices with the chicken livers and spoon over any pan juices. Garnish with watercress and wedges of grilled red onion.

A simple starter to prepare before a main course of roast guinea fowl with port gravy.

FLAT MUSHROOMS ON LINGUINI

SERVES 4

4 large flat mushrooms, wiped
   and stalks removed
40 g/1½ oz butter, melted
salt and pepper
175 g/6 oz fresh linguini
   or fine spaghetti
1 tablespoon walnut oil
2 tablespoons roughly chopped
   flat-leaf parsley

Roquefort sauce
125 g/4 oz Roquefort cheese
3 tablespoons fromage frais
juice of ½ orange
½ tablespoon coarsegrain
   mustard

Preheat the grill to its highest setting.

Place the mushrooms, gills side down, on a chopping board and slice through each mushroom, but do not separate the slices. Using a fish slice or palette knife, carefully transfer the mushrooms on to a baking sheet. Using the palm of your hand, gently flatten each mushroom to fan the slices. Spoon over the melted butter and season well. Grill the mushrooms for 6–8 minutes or until tender and golden brown.

Meanwhile, cook the pasta until just tender.

In a small bowl, blend the Roquefort, fromage frais, orange juice and mustard until smooth. Season to taste.

Drain the pasta well and toss with the walnut oil and parsley. Using a large spoon and fork, twist the pasta into four portions on individual plates. Top each pile of pasta with a fanned mushroom and a generous spoonful of the Roquefort sauce. Serve at once.

This would be a good prelude to a supper of chicken roasted with lemons and thyme, accompanied by a crisp green herby salad.

GAZPACHO SALAD

SERVES 4–6

4 ripe plum tomatoes, diced
175 g/6 oz red seedless
    grapes, halved
¼ cucumber, finely chopped
1 red pepper, finely chopped
juice of 1 lemon
2 teaspoons chilli sauce
    or to taste
salt and pepper

To serve
225 g/8 oz curd cheese
1 tablespoon plain yogurt
2 tablespoons fresh basil leaves
granary toast

In a bowl, combine all the salad ingredients together, season well and set aside.

Beat the curd cheese with the yogurt and season with black pepper. Spread the cheese mixture over the base of four serving plates. Spoon the gazpacho salad over the cheese, scatter with the basil leaves and serve with crisp granary toast.

Keep to the Spanish theme with a main course of paella or any hot shellfish dish.

ORIENTAL BROTH

SERVES 4

Stock

2 skinless, boneless chicken
    breasts, cut into fine strips
2 teaspoons chopped
    lemongrass
grated zest and juice of 1 lime
1 bay leaf
5 cm/2 inch piece of fresh
    ginger, grated
1 garlic clove, crushed
3 tablespoons light soy sauce
2 teaspoons unsweetened
    desiccated coconut
1.2 litres/2 pints water

To finish

1 large carrot, cut into fine strips
1 bunch of spring onions, cut
    into strips
50 g/2 oz mangetout, cut into
    fine strips
50 g/2 oz thin rice noodles or
    egg noodles
salt and pepper

Place all the stock ingredients in a large saucepan, bring to the boil and simmer for 15 minutes.

Add the carrot, spring onions, mangetout and noodles and simmer for a further 5–6 minutes or until the noodles are just tender.

Season to taste, ladle the soup into large soup bowls and serve at once.

Serve as part of an Oriental feast, with other dishes such as prawn satay with cashew sambal and green vegetable curry with fragrant rice. Finish with caramelized bananas and cinnamon ice cream.

SALAMI RAVIGOTTE

SERVES 4

225 g/8 oz Italian salami
2 tablespoons Greek black olives,
     pitted and roughly chopped
2 tablespoons baby caper berries
2 tablespoons virgin olive oil
1 shallot, very finely chopped
1 tablespoon fresh thyme leaves
juice of ½ lemon
pepper

Roasted tomatoes
25 g/1 oz butter, melted
1 plump garlic clove, crushed
½ teaspoon sugar
4 plum tomatoes, halved
     horizontally

Preheat the oven to 200°C/400°F/Gas Mark 6.

Arrange the salami on one large platter or four individual serving plates.

In a bowl combine the olives, capers, olive oil, shallot and thyme. Season with the lemon juice and black pepper. Set aside.

For the roasted tomatoes, combine the melted butter, garlic and sugar. Place the tomato halves on a baking sheet. Spoon the garlic butter over the tomatoes and place in the oven for 15–20 minutes, until softened and lightly charred, but still holding their shape.

To serve, spoon the olive mixture over the salami and serve at once with the warm tomatoes.

After this vibrant first course, I might serve a spinach and ricotta tart and a dessert of fresh dates with sweet white wine.

MEZZE PLATE

SERVES 4

175 g/6 oz goats' cheese, chilled
virgin olive oil for drizzling
salt and pepper
4 large sprigs of mint
pitta bread

Aubergine caviar
1 aubergine
2 tablespoons virgin olive oil
1 garlic clove, crushed
juice of ½ lemon
1 thin slice of bread, plunged
    into cold water and well
    squeezed out

Lentil salad
400 g/14 oz can of green lentils,
    drained and rinsed
225 g/8 oz cherry tomatoes,
    halved
½ bunch of spring onions,
    finely chopped
2 tablespoons balsamic vinegar
3 tablespoons virgin olive oil

First make the aubergine caviar. Preheat the oven to 200°C/400°F/Gas Mark 6. Prick the aubergine all over with a fork and bake in the oven for 40 minutes or until soft. Cut the aubergine in half lengthways and scoop out the pulp. Put the pulp into a food processor or liquidizer together with the remaining caviar ingredients and purée until smooth. Season to taste and set aside.

Combine all the lentil salad ingredients in a bowl and season well.

Cut the chilled goats' cheese into four slices.

To serve, spoon a generous heap of lentil salad and aubergine caviar on to four large dinner plates. Top each plate with a round of goats' cheese and drizzle with olive oil and freshly ground black pepper. Garnish with fresh mint and serve with a wedge of warm pitta bread.

The flavours are evocative of the eastern Mediterranean. Continue the meal with barbecued or grilled fish or chicken, marinated with oil and herbs if you like, followed by fresh fruit served on crushed ice.

HONEYED DUCK
with papaya salsa

SERVES 4

1 tablespoon soy sauce
2 duck breasts, skin on
1 tablespoon clear honey
4 sprigs of basil

Papaya salsa

2 small papayas, peeled
   and diced
1 orange pepper, diced
½ bunch of spring onions,
   finely sliced
2 tablespoons olive oil
zest and juice 1 of orange
juice of ½ lime
salt and pepper

In a bowl, combine all the salsa ingredients together and set aside to allow the flavours to develop.

Preheat the grill to its highest setting.

Sprinkle the soy sauce over the duck skin and rub it in. Season with black pepper, then spread the skin with the honey. Reduce the grill to a medium heat and grill the breasts for 8–10 minutes or until the skin is browned and the duck is still slightly pink.

To serve, carve the duck breasts into thin slices and arrange on individual serving plates. Add a mound of fresh salsa and top with a sprig of basil.

Follow with a main course of salmon steaks with gingered lentils.

CRAB TARTS
with ginger pistou

SERVES 4

325 g/12 oz shortcrust pastry
8 cm/3 inch piece of fresh
  ginger, chopped
3 tablespoons flat-leaf parsley,
  plus extra to garnish
1 tablespoon sunflower oil
325 g/12 oz white crab meat
  (fresh or frozen)
2 egg yolks
4 tablespoons crème fraîche
salt and pepper

Oriental vinaigrette

3 tablespoons medium sherry
2 teaspoons finely chopped
  lemongrass
1 kaffir lime leaf (optional)
2 tablespoons dark soy sauce
1 garlic clove, finely chopped
1 green chilli, seeded and
  finely chopped
1 sprig of basil
juice of ½ lime
2 tablespoons fish sauce
3 tablespoons sunflower oil

Preheat the oven to 200°C/400°F/Gas Mark 6. Roll out the pastry and use to line four tartlet tins, 10 cm/ 4 inches in diameter. Bake blind (page 36), then reduce the oven temperature to 180°C/350°F/Gas Mark 4.

In a small food processor, blend the ginger, parsley and oil together until they form a paste. Spread on to the base of the tartlets. Flake the crab and place on top of the paste.

In a bowl, mix together the egg yolks and crème fraîche and season with black pepper. Spoon this mixture into the tarts and return to the oven for about 15 minutes or until just set.

For the vinaigrette, put the sherry, lemongrass, lime leaf, soy sauce, garlic, chilli and basil in a small saucepan and simmer gently for 2 minutes. Combine the lime juice, fish sauce and sunflower oil in a bowl and stir in the lemongrass mixture. Lift out the lime leaf and basil and season to taste.

To serve, place each tart in the centre of a large plate, scatter parsley leaves around the tart and spoon the warm dressing over the leaves. Serve at once.

Follow with more spicy Oriental flavours, such as stir-fried Szechwan beef.

The Basics

THE LUXURY LARDER

Stocking up with basics such as pasta, rice, couscous, bulgar wheat, canned tomatoes and pulses is of course important, but to be even more creative in the kitchen, lavish your larder with ingredients that have intense flavours. Anchovies, smoked mussels and oysters, capers, olives, tapenade, sun-dried tomatoes, chillies and dried mushrooms, for example, will give added kick to everyday dishes. Each time you shop for basics add a couple of luxury storecupboard items to your list.

USE AND STORAGE OF OILS

Cold-pressed or virgin oils are oils from the first pressing, not only from olives, but also from nuts and sunflower and sesame seeds. These oils are becoming more widely available, and although they are expensive they are worth every penny for their intensity of flavour. Cold-pressed oils are at their best in dressings or in dishes where their flavour will not be overpowered or overheated. Store all oils with the lids on tightly, out of direct sunlight and in a cool place, but not in the refrigerator.

SPICES

It's always best to buy and store spices as whole seeds or pods, as they keep their aroma far longer. Grind them as you need them using a pestle and mortar or a coffee grinder. Failing that a chopping board and heavy saucepan, although this is hard work and not as effective! Ground spices have a shorter life, so buy in smaller quantities to be used within a month or so. Keep spices in an airtight container, in a cool place and out of direct sunlight.

A WORD ON
FRESH HERBS

Think of herbs as an ingredient rather than as a last-minute accessory and use them in abundance. For maximum flavour, use them roughly torn or coarsely chopped, or even left whole. Keep herbs fresh in the refrigerator, damp in plastic bags, or wrapped in moist paper towels. Big bunches of herbs can be kept in a little water like flowers, but keep out of direct sunlight.

BAKING BLIND

Tarts and quiches should be baked 'blind' or empty, to ensure a crisp crust for the finished dish.

• Roll out the pastry on a lightly floured board or work surface. To line the tart tin, roll the pastry loosely around the rolling pin, then unroll it over the tin. Press the pastry gently into the edge of the tin, then trim off excess pastry.

• Prick the base of the pastry with a fork and line with a circle of greaseproof paper, just large enough to cover the base and sides of the tart.

• Sprinkle in some uncooked rice, pasta or dried beans – just enough to cover the base of the tart. Too much will prevent the pastry from cooking.

• Leave the pastry to rest in the refrigerator for at least 20 minutes, using this time to preheat the oven.

• Bake in a hot oven until the pastry is almost cooked, removing the paper and rice for the last 5 minutes.

Zesting Citrus Fruits

When grating the zest of citrus fruits, make sure you get as much zest as possible by using a dry pastry brush to brush all the zest out of the grater.

Classic Cooking

STARTERS

Lesley Waters A former chef and now a popular television cook, appearing regularly on *Ready Steady Cook* and *Can't Cook Won't Cook*. Author of several cookery books.

VEGETABLE SOUPS

Elisabeth Luard Cookery writer for the *Sunday Telegraph Magazine* and author of *European Peasant Food* and *European Festival Food*, which won a Glenfiddich Award.

GOURMET SALADS

Sonia Stevenson The first woman chef in the UK to be awarded a Michelin star, at the Horn of Plenty in Devon. Author of *The Magic of Saucery* and *Fresh Ways with Fish*.

FISH AND SHELLFISH

Gordon Ramsay Chef/proprietor of London's Aubergine restaurant, recently awarded its second Michelin star, and author of Glenfiddich Award–winning *A Passion for Flavour*.

CHICKEN, DUCK AND GAME

Nick Nairn Chef/patron of Braeval restaurant near Aberfoyle in Scotland, whose BBC-TV series *Wild Harvest* was last summer's most successful cookery series, accompanied by a book.

LIVERS, SWEETBREADS AND KIDNEYS

Simon Hopkinson Former chef/patron at London's Bibendum restaurant, columnist and author of *Roast Chicken and Other Stories* and *The Prawn Cocktail Years*.

VEGETARIAN

Rosamond Richardson Author of several vegetarian titles, including *The Great Green Cookbook* and *Food from Green Places*.

PASTA

Joy Davies One of the creators of *BBC Good Food Magazine*, she has been food editor of *She, Woman* and *Options* and written for the *Guardian*, *Daily Telegraph* and *Harpers & Queen*.

CHEESE DISHES

Rose Elliot The UK's most successful vegetarian cookery writer and author of many books, including *Not Just a Load of Old Lentils* and *The Classic Vegetarian Cookbook*.

POTATO DISHES

Patrick McDonald Former chef/patron of the acclaimed Epicurean restaurant in Cheltenham, and food consultant to Sir Rocco Forte Hotels.

BISTRO

Anne Willan Founder and director of La Varenne Cookery School in Burgundy and West Virginia. Author of many books and a specialist in French cuisine.

ITALIAN

Anna Del Conte Author of several books on Italian food, including *The Gastronomy of Italy*, *Secrets from an Italian Kitchen* and *The Classic Food of Northern Italy* (chosen as the 1996 Guild of Food Writers Book of the Year).

Vietnamese

Nicole Routhier One of the United States' most popular cookery writers, her books include *Cooking Under Wraps*, *Nicole Routhier's Fruit Cookbook* and the award-winning *The Foods of Vietnam*.

Malaysian

Jill Dupleix One of Australia's best known cookery writers and broadcasters, with columns in the *Sydney Morning Herald* and *Elle*. Her books include *New Food* and *Allegro al dente*.

Peking Cuisine

Helen Chen Author of *Chinese Home Cooking*, she learned to cook traditional Peking dishes from her mother, Joyce Chen, the *grande dame* of Chinese cooking in the United States.

Stir-fries

Kay Fairfax A writer and broadcaster whose books include *100 Great Stir-fries*, *Homemade* and *The Australian Christmas Book*.

Noodles

Terry Durack Australia's most widely read restaurant critic and co-editor of the *Sydney Morning Herald Good Food Guide*. He is the author of *YUM*, a book of stories and recipes.

North Indian Curries

Pat Chapman Founded the Curry Club in 1982. A regular broadcaster on television and radio, he is the author of 20 books, which have sold more than 1 million copies.

Grills and Barbecues

Brian Turner Chef/patron of Turner's in Knightsbridge and one of Britain's most popular food broadcasters; he appears frequently on *Ready Steady Cook*, *Food and Drink* and many other television programmes.

Summer and Winter Casseroles

Anton Edelmann Maître Chef des Cuisines at the Savoy Hotel, London. Author of six cookery books, he has also appeared on television.

Traditional Puddings

Tessa Bramley Chef/patron of the acclaimed Old Vicarage restaurant in Ridgeway, Derbyshire and author of *The Instinctive Cook*.

Decorated Cakes

Jane Asher Author of several cookery books and a novel. She has also appeared in her own television series, *Jane Asher's Christmas* (1995).

Favourite Cakes

Mary Berry One of Britain's leading cookery writers, her numerous books include *Mary Berry's Ultimate Cake Book*. She has made many television and radio appearances.

Ice Creams and Semi Freddi

Ann and Franco Taruschio Owners of the renowned Walnut Tree Inn near Abergavenny in Wales, soon to appear in a television series, *Franco and Friends: Food from the Walnut Tree*. They have written three books together.

Text © Lesley Waters 1997

Lesley Waters has asserted her right to be identified
as the author of this Work.

Photographs © Philip Wilkins 1997

First published in 1997 by
George Weidenfeld & Nicolson
The Orion Publishing Group
Orion House
5 Upper St Martin's Lane
London WC2H 9EA

British Library Cataloguing-in-Publication data
A catalogue record for this book is available from
the British Library

ISBN 0 297 82335 3

Designed by Lucy Holmes
Edited by Maggie Ramsay
Food styling by Louise Pickford
Typesetting by Tiger Typeset